The Servant

The Servant

BY

Charles Lazenby, B.A.

1920

ORPHEUS PUBLISHING HOUSE
42 GEORGE STREET
EDINBURGH

 CLEAN Life, an open Mind, a pure Heart, an eager Intellect, an unveiled Spiritual Perception, a Brotherliness for all, a readiness to give and receive Advice and Instruction, ... a courageous Endurance of Personal Injustice, a brave Declaration of Principles, a valiant Defence of those who are unjustly attacked, and a constant eye to the Ideal of Human Progression and Perfection which the Secret Science depicts —These are the Golden Stairs up the Steps of which the Learner may climb to the Temple of Divine Wisdom. ::

Extract from the Teachings of H.P.B.

Proem

NIGHT reigned throughout the world and men slept. At the window of a humble cottage stood a child and watched a great silver star glittering in the cold blue eastern sky. He had just awakened to the wonder of himself, and the possibilities of self-expression seemed boundless. He was thinking of the many things he should like to do and be. While he thus followed his vagrant fancies, it seemed that the star moved closer to him, and became no longer a star but a radiant man who smiled upon him with such glorious love that the child's heart leaped with joy   The man took the child in his arms, filling him with happiness and a sense of unlimited power   The man spoke : " My little one, I will be with you always, to give you whatever your imagination finds most fair, and you, yourself, shall always make the choice   What of all things would you like most ? "

" I will be rich."

The star-man smiled and went his way.

The child was born into a world of unbounded wealth. Great heaps of gold, and coffers filled with precious jewels were his. He lived in palaces of white marble on the shores of sunny seas   A myriad slaves bowed to his bidding. In magnificent and golden splendour he passed, on pompous ships from land to land   Kings were his friends, and the world's great men hailed him as patron   He loaned money to monarchs, and was a power behind the destiny of nations—and he became weary and slept

Again the star-man came to him and bade him choose anew.

" I will be a warrior-king "

His guardian smiled and went his way

He was born to opportunity which he grasped   He became the leader of vast armies, and as he rode down the long ranks they saluted him with trust and fealty   He led them to war and in the brunt of many battles won his way to greatness. He owned vast dominions. His flag flew over high and low as a symbol of conquering power. Nations feared his name. Lesser kings gave tribute to him. His navy was supreme in many seas. He changed geography and laid the foundation of a new history—and he was weary and slept.

When the star-soul came to him, the child said   " I will be a great priest and a power in religion "

His guardian smiled and went his way.

The child found himself in a cloister, through the walls of which came no sound of the weary world   It was a fair life and he joyed in the sense of power which vigils and the practice of ascetic exercises gave to him. He hated sin   He watched the burning of the yellow candles, and knelt in adoration before the symbols of his faith   He worshipped his God in the fulness of his ideal, and was crowned a saint by a host of admiring followers   Each word from his lips stung the sinner like a whip and the branding-iron was ever in his hand to put an unchanging scar on all the wicked   He appointed himself of God to judge and condemn the evil   He rose in power until the highest office of the religion was his, and his words were looked upon by millions as the words of God Himself   He served his God well, and was very weary and slept

When his guardian came the child told him that he was weary of suppression, and chose to have a full sensuous life   His lover smiled and went his way.

He entered a world abundant in promise of pleasure   Perfumes filled the air. Flutes and harps blended with bird-songs   Houris of paradise, filled with longing, ministered voluptuously to the measure of his desire   In the hot and languid air of gorgeous coloured courts, sinuous dancers moved to erotic melodies   Banquet followed banquet with the choicest wines, most luscious fruits, most savoury viands   Rich silks and velvets were his garment, and he lay at ease on couches of eiderdown, between pillars of exquisitely carved ivory—and he was weary and slept

During that day there had passed through his courts a girl, who, while understanding and not scorning the life he led, was yet not attracted to sensuousness, unless as the expression of a deeper life-purpose   She had smiled quizzically and comprehendingly at him, much as a mother might smile at the play of a child, but had gone from him leaving her imprint on his memory   When the star-man came the child said—" I will have the appearance of those qualities which will make this girl desire and love me "   The guardian smiled and went his way

In a simpler and less stimulating life the girl met him, and although he had in no essential changed, yet through environment he had altered his outward seeming, and the girl loved and deified him, and offered him the depths of her pure womanhood. He shrank back and knew he was unworthy of this gift—and he slept.

Now, when his guardian came, his first thought was of the girl, but he said—" I will be a great scientist, and have extended knowledge of many facts." The Master smiled and went his way

The child was born with an amazing curiosity, and into a body vibrant with health and having a fine brain. He saw the world as a vast and convenient hall, the walls of which had many doors leading to other halls In the centre of each hall was a great chest of drawers, each drawer filled with facts. A few of the drawers were orderly, but in most the facts were in chaos, and needed patient intelligence to bring them into harmony, and show them forth for observation. He was filled with enthusiasm, and began eagerly sorting the disordered facts. He set in array the facts in a number of drawers, classified them and put his name upon them The crowd passing through the hall glanced carelessly into the cases and spoke with awe of the great accomplishments of our student His energy led him into several halls, and he was acclaimed one of the world's great scientists. He looked back into the hall he had first entered, and found that his youthful achievements were covered with dust, while many new drawers were in as great disorder as ever—and he was weary and slept.

The child longed greatly for his girl companion, yet when his guardian came, the choice was made to see the beauty of the world, and show forth the beauty that he saw. The star-man smiled and went his way.

Beauty shone about him everywhere. He heard the harmony of a myriad mixing sounds—the cricket's hum, the purl of the brook, the laughter of men and women, the cries of the city streets, the tones of the thunder, and the tinkling of million rain-drops He composed great musical works, uplifting and thrilling emotions He saw the beauty of form and colour in all the objects around him, and was able to show it forth for others He knew beauty, and whether working with pigments, marble, or words, he was able to give a plenitude of joy to all who came before the things he produced He was a master

of fine arts, and was a genius for his own and coming generations—
and he was weary and slept.

Then the girl called him with an irresistible call, and he prayed to
be made worthy of her. His guardian smiled and went his way.

They lived and worked together, and each watched with the growth
of new insight the awakening of responsibility to a wider purpose
They fulfilled, completed, and made fruitful each the life of the other,
and watched with joy the increase of that love which destroys attachments and leaves the soul free from all bondage This day dawned,
and when the star-man came each chose the destiny nearest to his
heart. The child whose destiny we have followed through all these
lives said—" I am very weary of life, and the *ennui* of all ideas is
through my soul. I can think of nothing I desire, nor any state
among men that I would fain fill, I see nothing that can give me
real pleasure. I know I cannot die. If there is one ideal towards
which mankind is tending, let me serve that and help my fellow man
I feel very old , let me then through all my coming days serve mankind as they most need me   I do not know what is best for man in
the far-flung purpose of life, but I know that all is well and that he
moves towards a destiny fine and noble   Let me not depart from him
while he needs any to help him   Let me be an instrument in any
environment for his unfolding. I do not ask that my service should
be seen by him, nor do I care which fellow-man I serve, since all men
move to the same great goal   Take me to serve where I am most
needed. I can picture no reward, or, even if I could, I am weary of all
rewards. Let me become a servant of man."

The Master said—" This choice, my child, is different from the
others   In what you are now choosing you will stand alone. You
will not be seen by men as great or wise   You will never have wealth,
for what money comes to you must belong to the race, never to yourself   You may not have houses nor fine clothes, nor always even
enough to eat. You will strive to aid men, and they will laugh at your
efforts   You will see them constantly thinking and acting in ways
to bring pain and sorrow upon themselves and will be powerless to
prevent them, though you must always help them when the pain has
become manifest   You will wander up and down in the world and
will seldom meet those who are serving as you are   You will have no
one place to call home   You will have no special friends, for you will

be the servant of all men, and the world's friendship is never of this
kind You will be lonely and will have the sorrow of men you have
never heard of, nor will ever meet, at least for ages, placed on your
shoulders. You are a soldier enlisting for rough service in a war
which will continue until the last of the human race has ceased to need
help. There is little in this which you wish to undertake that men
desire. Nothing will belong to you Your whole being may be used
in the most unpleasant tasks Life after life you will be sent among
those who most need help, whether it is pleasant to you to go or not.
Your loyalty to this ideal you choose, will be tested in a thousand ways.
You will undergo stern discipline and little commendation will be
given to you Your general will more often reprimand you than
praise you Your sacrifice of personal aims will not appear at all
remarkable, since every private in the ranks has done the same Each
life you will suffer and gain wide experience, that you may have a complete sympathy with all men You will know sorrow and woe, you
will shrink in fear, you will receive no reward but the love which you
must continually pour forth Think well before you choose this path."

The child said—" There is no other."

In the radiance of his gladness the star-soul took the child in his
arms, and bore him afar. The child felt a wonderful peace steal over
his senses and his mind. Great worlds of undreamed-of splendour
burst upon his vision. Vast chords of marvellous music filled the
infinite spaces, through which in rhythmical flight flowed mighty
glowing presences. The highest ecstasy of earth was intensified a
thousand times. Absolute freedom of perfect joy was everywhere in
that high world The child lay in complete happiness on the bosom
of his star guide. Then his guardian spoke and said—" This world is
yours, you have thrown off the trammels of earthly desire, no more
are you called upon to bear physical limitations You have won the
right to this birthright No pain enters this world, nor will its joy
pall as do those of the earth you have left You will move in the glory
of your divine inheritance for which your earth-lives were ordained,
and be free from all memory of sorrow, or pain, or fear. You will
forget, as you are now forgetting, that there is a world of struggling
mortals who were your kin The sorrow of the world will pass from
you and you will remember it no more, but among men that pain is
real. Few there are who, seeing this world, still wish to make the

choice you were making   There is no question of right or wrong in
this matter   This world is your birthright ; it is your true home.
It is perfectly right that you should stay here, and the High Rulers
will approve your choice if you so decide   All men will reach this
joy in the course of the ages whether you return or not.   If you do
go down it will be to help them in their suffering, and to help them
forward into this realm of peace, and beauty, and light ''

The bright guide took the child down into the slums of great
cities, into the prisons, asylums, and workhouses, among the out-
casts of civilization, and among those who preyed greedily upon
their kind , into the lowest dens of vice where the bodies of men and
women were placed at auction, into the haunts of squalor and sordid
meanness.   He showed him all the pettiness, and the small and
pitiful aims which guided most human action   The guide said—
"These are thy brethren, and they will need thy aid for milleniums.
By nearly all their thoughts they are bringing suffering upon themselves, which you must willingly share for the love you bear them.
Now, my child, choose ''

The child said—"I will be a servant of mankind ''

The Master smiled and went his way.

■ ■ ■ ? ;

Introduction

The Earthworm becomes a Butterfly, the Butterfly marries the Rose,—and the Raven is born —*Crazy Proverb*

BY way of introduction a few definitions may be of worth. Black Magic is the use of the powers latent in man for his own development, and in the use of which he is willing to sacrifice the well-being of other human beings By his own development is meant any sensuous, emotional or mental expansion of personality at the sacrifice of others and with indifference to their good. An ordinary undeveloped man who takes advantage of another's weakness and ignorance to gain some fancied advantage, in money or the gratification of some personal ambition, is treading the path, which, if followed, as his deeper and fuller powers develop will make of him a Black Magician.

White Magic is the use of all these powers for the well-being of humanity, and in the use of which the man who uses them is continually willing to sacrifice his own personal comforts and ambitions for the good of mankind He will forego gladly the pleasures of the senses and that recognition of his personality which he might claim, if by this denial he sees that mankind will be aided and helped forward on the long journey towards the goal of human perfection.

Left-Hand Magic is the use of the powers of one's own being plus ceremonial, also to build body or organisation or form, for the life to manifest It is the throwing outward into concreteness the form, whether physical, as expressed in the cultivation of the senses,—or in the building of organisations to be used as the vehicles for ideals, religious, scientific, political, artistic, or any other conception which requires an organised form for its manifestation It is form-building, and its function is not so much concerned with the life and nature of the ideal as to build the form for its expression

Right-Hand Magic is the use of the inner powers of man's nature to overcome the limitations and bondage of form, and to free his soul from all the trammels of sensation and the emotions and imaginations which tend to tie him to non-permanent aspects of life It is the service of his eternal and immortal part in which the mortal and transitory forms are sacrificed and their seductions conquered

The Higher Magic is the conscious use of the powers and forces latent and developed from within. In its expression it seeks no outer aid of ceremonial or religious organisation   It cultivates a positive will, and by concentration of the mind enables the man to become a creator of new values, and a powerful centre of thought, emotion, and magnetism.

The Lower Magic is the use of auxiliary aids to the expression of man's desires and ambitions, and to the making more stable and objective his mental conceptions   It does not aid the spiritual unfoldment, but quickens the emotional and magnetic fields of his personality   All chants, invocations, evocations, the sciences of the use of mantra, of colour, of incense, and of the magnitisation of food, human forms, and other material objects is part of its sphere   The lower magician also understands the use of his own magnetic force, and may if he chooses devitalise and envitalise those around him, though this practice carries with it such responsibility that no truly instructed adept will care to do it   Lawyers addressing juries, directors of joint-stock companies, committee men in the labour world, revivalists in religious gatherings, often use unconsciously these magnetic forces and win their way for a time at the expense of those associated with them   It is, however, destructive to the practitioner, and in the Aryan occultism is avoided by the initiate.   For the same reason hypnotism and mesmerism or any control of passive types from the astral or from the physical planes of consciousness is practically forbidden in the Aryan lodges.

The reader will pardon a few more definitions.

The Manu of humanity is that limitation within the Universal Mind which contains all the ideals and conceptions relating to man and his evolution from the infant and undeveloped state to his perfection at the end of the complete cycle of human growth

There are seven great departments of humanity, and seven divisions of conscious purpose within each of these great departments.   Each of these forty-nine sub-departments is evolving the types within it, and educating its members in its own particular lessons.

The work of the first three root-races or great departments is finished, and we do not need to consider them in this book   There remain at present fourteen sub-races of man to be considered, however, and the needs of these varying types should be studied by any occultist who in the Theosophical Society seeks to serve the ideal of Universal Brotherhood without any distinctions of race, creed, sex, caste or colour

The White Lodge is made up of the Servants of Man. No one is a member whose life is not dedicated to human service. Each member is pledged to aid humanity in its long journey, and to the teaching of man in all departments the lessons suited to his unfoldment at that point. The least developed man is important, and his needs must be considered by the true lover of man. Because there are fourteen departments of human life, and indeed because each of these sub-races is again divided into seven grades or families—there are a corresponding number of divisions of the White Lodge, and over each family of the sub-race there watches and guides a group of the servants whose function is to protect and enlighten that particular field of human endeavour

The methods of instruction and the nature of the lessons to be learned are thus very diverse. The ideals are different, but all are necessary to the unfolding life of man

Wisdom is the right use of knowledge The knowledge must be acquired and assimilated Then it must be used for the helping of man. Any member of the human race who, having grasped the ideal, the conception of life suited to the next stage of human endeavour, brings into his or her life the projection of that ideal, becomes the embodiment of it, for whatsoever is sown in the heart and mind of man is reaped in physical action This person or these persons are then called Boddhisattvas—or wisdom embodiments—and in each of the various families of the sub-races of the root-races, there are, from time to time, embodiments of this character, who then become examples to the growing children of men.

Unscrupulous and selfish men in that family cluster around such a figure and strive to nullify its effect This may be done in various ways. They may teach their less individualised brethren that the Boddhisattva is far out of all reach of example—they may make of him a god for worship, thus violently disassociating him from the practical life and needs of those to whom he came,—or they may kill him, distort or destroy his words, or put words into his mouth suited to their own selfish ends, the spirit of which is absolutely contrary to his purpose and ideal.

Part of the function of the members of the White Lodge is to protect the ideal from these priesthoods of outer religion, the Herods who seek the young child's life to destroy it.   The Boddhisattva is thus preserved as an ideal for coming ages in spite of the priesthoods of selfishness, who, finding the ideal has slipped from their throttling fingers, build churches and temples to it, and like spiders in the midst of their web, suck the blood from the flies, their less selfish brethren, who would approach to partake of the honey of the ideal shown forth by the Boddhisattva.

One or two more definitions and the introduction will be complete

An occultist may be either a student of the hidden lore or a magician using his knowledge of the forces in man and nature in the outer and inner worlds.

The occult student may be selfish or unselfish.   He may be seeking for self-development by practices of control over the various elements of his soul, or he may be seeking the kingdom of heaven in the hearts of all men, and striving to make it manifest in himself by continual loving deeds and constant kindly thoughts   In the latter case he will soon know that all the powers and riches of life will be added unto him without taking thought or care for them.

The occult students thus fall into two classes—the seekers for knowledge and the seekers for usefulness, and the progress and development is very different for them as they go forward.   This little book is not written for the seekers for knowledge, so if such are now reading it they may put it down.   If, however, there are those who desire to help their fellow-man in his ignorance and be-wilderment, and would develop the powers and capacities of their souls for this purpose and towards this end, this writing may prove of value.   It is intended to be a *resumé* of the Rules and Discipline for all those who would seek the condition of Servitude to the " blind orphan " humanity, and who wish to develop their souls as instruments in the hands of the Universal Wisdom for man's betterment.   These rules, if practised, will make of the candidate a member of the White Lodge, and bring him or her into association with the Servants who for ages have been dedicating their lives and bodies to human well-being

THESE rules are laid down for those who wish to meet and know the Masters of Wisdom who watch over and protect the evolving life of man   There is a lodge composed of dedicated servants of the Supreme Life under Its human form in all nations and tribes. This Life is one, and is the Light in every human heart   The saviours of men are those members of the White Lodge who from time to time come forward into the outer life of humanity to reveal the true path and point the way, which, if any man will follow, he may save himself from ignorance and folly, and may attain the clarity of perception which enables him to transcend the limits of his mortality and to dwell consciously in immortality

■ ■ ■ ■ ■

RULE I.

The first step is to live to benefit and serve mankind —
H. P BLAVATSKY, " *Voice of the Silence* "

THIS step may be taken at any time, in any condition of mind, and under any conceivable circumstance   One thing only is essential —the ideal of human service must really appeal to the man or woman who dedicates his life, and he must have a sincere desire to serve his fellowman   It is not necessary that he shall believe in God, in the Masters of Wisdom, in a Supreme Architect, or in the Hosts of the Builders , he may be a materialist, an atheist or an agnostic ; he may be irreligious and cynical ; he may look upon all religion as merely credulity and superstition ,—yet, if he desire to help mankind to a higher and happier, a more intellectual and self-reliant condition, he may pledge himself to this ideal of human betterment and in so doing he will take this first step towards Wisdom   He must be willing to work for the ideal of human well-being as he himself conceives it, and to sacrifice his personal aims and pleasures to some extent in this cause.

This first step is, however, curious in that it never comes to an end,—that is—the movement of its initial impulse continues while all succeeding steps are being taken.

Some simple dedication, made in the silence and secrecy of the inner n... will b... m... h... fui v hose pledge is given to what he

conceives to be his better and nobler Self, to support It in Its outer
action   He need not comprehend himself as one aspect of Universal
Consciousness, the Lord of Life who is in and through all thoughts,
actions and forms in the Cosmos   This Knowledge will come later.
The importance of the dedication is to impress strongly the life force
of the aspirant with a tendency in the right direction   It also gives
stability and makes concretely objective the ideal to which the life
is given.

Each, according to his own temperament, artistic, religious,
exuberant, phlegmatic, or practical, may say the following—or
something equivalent :—He may put his body in any posture he
pleases, he may cover his self-consciousness with laughter or a " cuss,"
or he may kneel in devotion at his bedside.   These things are excres-
cences and do not affect the result one way or another , providing
always that the one dedicating is sincere in what he says.

DEDICATION.

*I here and now, with all that I am of weakness and of strength, offer
myself in all my thoughts, emotions, sensations, aspirations, volitions
and actions, to the service of my fellowman   May this ideal, from this
moment guide and direct me, mould and educate me, that my life may
become an embodiment of it.   May all my forces, capacities and inherent
possibilities be developed to this end.   I will to give myself wholly to
the ideal of human well-being*

*   *   *   *   *   *   *   *

If you are religious you may personify your ideal thus stated as
the Lord of Life, the Ideal Lover, but in so doing be careful not to
externalise It. Do not make of It any outer being. This may be
done in exoteric religion alone, but not by a student in the occult
Mysteries.   For you it would be a grave error.   You are striving to
form inwardly the Ideal and all religious externalization of it, all
anthropomorphising, tends to substitute false appearances for the
Reality   The worship of external conceptions of the All-Life may
be valuable to the great mass of uninstructed mankind, but as H P B.
says (page 300, vol I *Secret Doctrine*)—Every occultist is a Nastika
—one who rejects idols, including every anthromorphic god   The
Secret Doctrine admits a Logos, a Demiurge, an Architect, but that
Demiurge is no personal deity—therefore neither the collective Host

(Demiurge) nor any of the working Powers individually, are proper subjects for divine honours or worship All are entitled to the grateful reverence of humanity, however, and man ought to be ever striving to help the divine evolution of *Ideas* by becoming, to the best of his ability, a *co-worker with Nature* in the cyclic task The ever-unknowable Karana alone, the Causeless Cause of all causes, should have its shrine and altar on the holy and ever-untrodden ground of our heart—invisible, intangible, unmentioned, save through the " still, small voice " of our spiritual consciousness. Those who worship before it ought to do so in the silence and the sanctified solitude of their Souls ; making their Spirit the sole mediator between them and the Universal Spirit, their good actions the only priests.

Remember, you are a servant of man From now on keep this thought like a torch burning steadily in the forefront of your consciousness. Look around you and you will see two types of occult students One group striving to develop capacity to carry them to higher levels of self-development, the other group to which you belong, may be simply called " The Servants." Both types are legitimate. As one of the former class develops his intellectual and synthetic power, unless he wilfully put himself against the current of normal evolution and choose to become a black magician—he will find himself by his own insight and knowledge, using his powers and increased capacities for the well-being of his fellows. You, a servant, on the other hand, as you are sincere and earnest in your desire to help mankind, will find yourself hungry for knowledge, and be willing to undergo the strictest discipline, if necessary, that you may become more efficient.

It is recorded by a sage that both paths lead to the same goal, although at the beginning they appear to go in diverse ways. Each path has on it its own difficulties and obstacles to be overcome. On the path of self-development the student meets the following obstructions :—Pride, vanity, the temptations of external pomp, the insignia of orders, priesthoods and fraternities, the conventional conceptions of outer groups of comrades, the apparent ease of attainment to certain coveted positions, titles, honours, acclamations, visible successes, social position, wealth, the recognition of an applauding audience and the approval and favour of those in high places. Those tempt him from his soul's task and hinder sometimes for lives, the true progress and deeper purpose of the seeker

You also will find your special difficulties Pride and vanity are common to both paths. The desire for recognition, which is legitimate as a reward for those on the self-culture path, is forbidden to you You must act each day as the ideal dictates without thought of either reward or punishment For following what you consider right you must be indifferent to the approval or censure of any. Look constantly to the guidance of the wiser and deeper Self, the voice in the silence of your own heart. Do not strive for your own development as such, or think too much about it. Forget it so far as you can in thinking of the well-being of those around you Cultivate humility in its truest sense and then in whatever environment your work lies you will fulfil the task capably and well, and you will have far less to overcome than if you allow self-assertiveness in any of its forms to develop within you.

The Kingdom of Heaven is a state of consciousness within, and you must strive to bring it into evidence in all the lives near you. You do not find it by looking within your own personality, but by seeing it as the heritage of every man and woman of the race, and trying to make it apparent in their lives Because it is within all, it is also within yourself Seek ye first the uncovering of this quality in others and you will know it in yourself

. . . . .

RULE II.

Be continuous in your dedication to human service.

IN order to form a tendency, or thought habit (the Sanscrit word is "Samskara"), which will automatically perform action according to the ideal impressed upon it, continuity is absolutely necessary This is true for all ideals It does not matter how high, noble, or attractive they may be, it is essential to clarify them in the mind by constant repetition In this way alone will they become objective and authoritative in your life Each morning and each evening you should draw yourself back to the central thought of the ideal of service to which your life is given.   This is one important form of concentration, and you should practise this consistently for seven years   You should never repeat it mechanically, but each time should think earnestly of the giving of yourself, both for learning and teaching, for receiving aid and helping   You will, in this way, knowing your dedication to be sincere, come to look upon yourself as a servant of mankind.   In this you must be humble.   Without pride and without arrogance you must do the little duties of your daily life   You must prepare your mind by the contemplation of the solidarity of the human family, for the larger duties and responsibilities which will unfold for you as you grow in knowledge   It will be well for most not to specialize too much during this first seven years, but think as widely as you can of the human problem in its total aspect, rather than in its departmental or national phases This advice, however, does not apply to all aspirants

. . . . .

RULE III.

Learn Discrimination.

As you have continually dedicated yourself to the service of man, you will have found yourself confronted with the problem as to what factors in your experience are permanent and eternal, and which, under the dominion of time, are impermanent and transient. As you solve this problem you will lay the true foundation on which you will later build your character.   You will help yourself in the cultivation of clearsightedness by frequently and thoughtfully repeating the following :—

I am not my physical body—but that which uses it.

I am not my emotions—but that which controls them

I am not my mental images—but that which creates them

My imaginations, emotions, and sensations are passing expressions of me, the Abiding Self.

I am in and through them, they are phases of Me but I remain apart—the Ordainer and the Seer.

Concentrate upon this statement, consider it well, grasp the truth contained within it, make of it a living reality in your life, and this third rule will carry you far in your quest for that knowledge which will enable you to help others.

Your personality, which you—the eternal Self—have offered to human service, is made up of seven characteristics which are subject to change and may be developed and modified   These are called "skandhas"   They are the following :—

1st —Your Four Bodies—Gross Physical, Finer Physical, Emotion-charged Imagination-body, and Imagination-body free from emotion

2nd —Your Sensations—visual, auditory, olfactory ; gustatory, sexual, tactile, including physical pain ; thermal, organic, etc

3rd —Your abstract conceptions of life, *i.e*, your ideas relating to religion, the state, the arts, moral standards of your time and place, your social position, etc.

4th —Your tendencies—that is the impulses arising, apparently spontaneously, to act in certain ways and to avoid action in others ; to think easily in certain directions and to find it almost impossible to form conceptions in others   These are what make you incline toward idealism, materialism, æstheticism, asceticism, logical thinking, etc.

5th —Your mental power—that is retentive memory, clear visualization, mathematical precision, etc.

6th.—Your heaven-forming power ("the kingdom of heaven is within you")—that is the power developed by kindly deeds and thoughts, by putting yourself out to make others comfortable and happy, by standing in the background and being glad to have others fill the best and most honoured places, etc

7th.—Your spiritual power—that is the capacity for universal vision, the loss of all sense of separation from the All-Life in the world of changing form   This is the power which enables you to say with absolute certainty and simplicity : "I and the Eternal Life are One."

To stand aside in your true and immortal consciousness and view the play of the three great nature forces—called the "gunas"—through the above seven characteristics, and to be unaffected by the actions and reactions of the qualities inherent in the fields of objective experience, is to have obtained the discrimination aimed at by the practice of Rule 3.

RULE IV.

Learn the value of concentration.

WISDOM has been defined by the master Hilarion as "the right use of knowledge "

Right usage presupposes a purpose and a plan.

In repeating the statement in Rule 3 you have been forced to take refuge in the Eternal, and will gradually free yourself from the thought that the non-permanent elements of your personality are the Immortal Self   You now come to see them in their true light as experiences of the Self.

As you come to the realization of your creative power in the world of thought, you will next wish to give stability and a greater permanence to the ideals in your mind. You will realize that all moral responsibility lies in the deeper regions of your mind and that it is what proceedeth forth from a man's heart that exalteth or defileth him. In order to give stability, then, you must learn and practise concentration. You cannot build your ideal of their well-being into the humanity of the future until that ideal has become clear and defined in your own mind, and this can only be done through concentration.

As a pure spring of water welling up and sending its refreshing streams down clear-cut channels, so does the Spirit in man well up and send its love and blessing through ideals fixed by concentration and made permanent in the mind

My advice to you, if you are a western student, is to avoid the breathing exercises laid down in so many books on concentration. They are dangerous, and unless one has a competent teacher close at hand are sure to do more harm than good. You will gain more by consistently picturing the ideal state of mankind and dwelling on it to the exclusion of all lesser ideals, than in years of Pranayama practice without ideality.

RULE V.

Practise Clear Thinking.

HAVING learned the value of concentration, you should train your mind to always think clearly and decisively upon every matter which comes to your attention. Get rid of cloudy, ambiguous, half-finished and inconclusive trains of thought. You will find that you have more of these than you know. One of the best means to attain to this mental clarity is the study of mathematics By concentration you have developed the art of fixing your attention upon one ideal and holding it positively, so that it remains undisturbed by all other mental images and unmoved by the fluctuating emotions The ideal for you of course is human service. Many adepts of the the White Lodge have insisted upon a study of mathematics as the best discipline, and as necessary to the understanding of the deeper problems of occultism , as, for instance, the evolutionary ratios, the co-relation of tattvic forces, the cyclic connections between races and nations, the astronomical calculations upon which the astrological impersonal inferences are based, the numerical values of the god names, their meaning and potency, and their relation to the chemical elements, the laws of physics and the various tanmatras.

The master Pythagoras particularly demands˜ of his disciples that definite and unemotional thinking which the study of mathematics alone gives. His pupils study algebra, trigonometry, plane and solid geometry, and astronomy.

Other masters and adepts, for the comprehension of whose ideals mathematics is necessary, and whose disciples are trained in this science are Serapis, Althotos, Astrologos, Trithemius, Khemi, and the great master of Agriculture—Triptolemus. It is interesting to note that although the master Hilarion does not specifically demand mathematics as a qualification in his disciples, yet tradition says that he himself was, in a nineteenth century incarnation and while still a very young man, the greatest mathematician in Europe.

RULE VI.

Follow your own ideal according to your temperament and development

SOME candidates—beautiful, gentle, and loving in their nature, but without intellectual cultivation—may feel discouraged on reading the foregoing rules   They may think the discipline too severe. Let such clearly realize that in the life of service there are many ideals and that all temperaments can be used.   To earnestly desire to serve mankind is much more important than to be a great mathematician lacking this ideal   In the earlier stages of the life of a disciple and perhaps for several lives, what capacity he may have, be it small or great, will never be refused by the Masters of Wisdom, but the love which makes him acceptable and valuable in the great task will quicken within him desire for that greater utility for which mathematical knowledge is essential   Therefore, let no discouragement fill your loving mind because you are not mathematical   The ability will come to you in time.

Intellectual development and a deeper love are paths which lead to the same goal.   They run side by side and must be travelled together   Love without intelligence is as a wind blown over the desert, but intellect without love is barren ; it produces nothing. These two together are Wisdom, and Wisdom is also the balanced forth-throwing into manifestation of ideals for the well-being of a whole class of divine objects   In the case of the White Brotherhood this class of divine objects is the total human family

Every Master of the White Lodge as he has stood on the threshold of his final surrender has taken the following pledge —

" *To the close of this great cycle I swear I shall not abandon man, that I shall not cease to create ideals for his betterment, to teach him lessons necessary for his growth, to help him to carry his heavy burdens and to quicken his aspirations at all stages of his development   I swear to continually pour out to him loving impulses, and from time to time to take part with him in those affairs which to him are important as his needs shall dictate   Until the last man shall have come to the realization of his true nature I shall not abandon him.   I shall not enter into the great bliss of Nirvana while any one of mankind, my brethren, needs my assistance* "

Such a pledge, of course, cannot be taken in the initial stages of discipleship, but you should fix your thought on this conception as you strive to form of yourself a perfect instrument in the world of personality for the Self to use.

. . . . .

RULE VII.
Do not compromise.

An outstanding and immutable law in the occult life of the servant is that when your pledge to human service is taken all the weakness and strength, not alone of yourself but of humanity, rise within your consciousness, testing you in many ways.   They tempt you to sacrifice the duty imposed upon you by this new ideal.   Pleasures of various kinds freely offer themselves to allure you to forgetfulness More subtly still, lesser duties, the expected conventional behaviour, the ideas of right and wrong held by friends and acquaintances, all the accustomed and habitual acquiesences in the valuation of life's problems—these to this time have been friendly to your advance You are now asked to revalue and discard some of them, certainly ; many of them, probably.   If the ideal of human service is a burning torch in your heart, it will demand that your evolution leap forward into the realm of a self-determination quite different from that of the average man, which you have ceased to be in taking your pledge

You are now in the condition of Arjuna at the beginning of his instructions as given in the Bhagavad Gita.   At this point and for some time it will be fatal for you to compromise or to follow any dharma—that is, ideal—other than that great one to which you have given your life

Not alone will pleasures tempt you to compromise, but also fears and aversions, the heritage of all your past will come from the shadowy region and take concrete form threatening you with pain, poverty, possibly ignominy, loneliness, and other conditions abhorrent to your personality

These allurements and intimidations both arise in your causal body ; that body of facts and memories relating to your whole progress through the human race and the storehouse of your ages of experience   Enticements and menaces both together form what is known as "THE GUARDIAN OF THE THRESHOLD." You must meet and overcome this before you can pass into the Temple of True Knowledge It may take years, it may take incarnations, or it may take one second to bring this battle to a successful conclusion, but before you can become an initiate of the White Brotherhood of human servants you must have come victorious through and above this strife

Do not, however, be dismayed by this, or think that you can be of no use to mankind until this task is accomplished. From the moment your dedication is taken, you become valuable in the work, and may do splendid service to man all through the battle

You must, however, determine never to compromise. Never allow yourself from fear or for pleasure to turn aside. Be one-pointed. " Let no image of the senses get between Its light and thine "

To aid you in this fray the following dedication may be helpful :—

" Supreme Lord of Life within me, and working through me into the world of men, let Thy great light shine clearly upon the ideal of human service to which I have pledged myself. Let no shadows hide it. According to the needs of mankind at this time, surround me with those conditions which will develop usefulness, whether these be of wealth or poverty, of sickness or health, of fame or disgrace, of high or low estate, of loneliness or sweet comradeship, of stirring activity or apparent inertia. I will to be a servant of mankind, and by Thee inwardly I will to be developed and shaped to fulfil this destiny Take me and use me.

■ ■ ■ ■ ■

RULE VIII.

Observe carefully the life around you, in relation to yourself, and strive to understand its mystery

By the time you reach this rule you will have entered into the life of occultism in earnest Now you are called upon to develop the double time-vision. You must accustom yourself to view the events of the passing days seeing them as parts of a time-sweep of thousands of years of racial growth. You must try to think in terms of ten thousand years and of the daily task simultaneously without letting your wider perspective detract from the immediate duty. In your larger seeing you must be free from personal emotion, prejudice or predeliction Yet the occultist is a man of affairs

Your life will be passed down among men, and you will appear to work with the same enthusiasm as do those who hold the limited vision. By you the building or the destruction of a nation—any nation,—or of the external form of a religion—any religion,—must be seen as merely part of the evolutionary plan, ordained, projected, and without mistake

You must know that through the anguish of spirit, so apparent in the common life of man, the winged flame burns brighter, and the race is carried to a higher level No cloud must blur the glorious vision of a perfect and loving purpose in a divine plan. With the eye of the god within, you must view the centuries Aye ! the millenniums, and with complete faith your intuition must reveal the meaning of the movements of war and peace, the rise and fall of nations and castes with their accompanying ideals Of necessity, with this vision you can have no bias , but as an onlooker of eternity, you must love all the children of men—nations, tribes and temperaments—good and bad, high and low, aristocratic and plebeian, cultured and crude, educated and ignorant, far-sighted and short-sighted,— personally ambitious and martyrs to an impersonal cause

You see now that every type is needed in the world ; that necessary lessons are being learned in each phase Every human being through the long series of his incarnate lives is developing, first the sense of personal identity, and then the power to use the identity in humanity's cosmic plan

While the above is true, you are not allowed to sit idly by saying, " All is well All is well The Lord of the Garden is wealthy in wisdom. He does not need my labour I have no personal part in the movements of the race "

If you do this your vision of the great things will quickly vanish , your life will become commonplace, and cynical scepticism may take the place of erstwhile grandeur

A plant in the garden of immensity, if you deny your part with the other flowers, you will quickly wilt and your beauty will fade

You will find yourself constantly called upon to decide in small matters and to definitely take sides in essentially unimportant controversies. " You must work as those do who are ambitious " And, withal, you must keep these two time elements absolutely distinct— the far vision and the present need.

The ancients pictured Hermes as a double statue, a young child and an old man. This was to signify that Widsom was childlike in its simplicity and faith, though hoary with the experience of myriad ages. It also shows the double vision of which I have been speaking

So in this eighth rule you are told to watch carefully the life around you This means you must observe it without arrogance, self-pride, personal ambition, ostentation, false humility, or any separative tendency of thought You are now a dedicated and accepted younger brother and as such you must remain one with the life of mankind Not apart from it, if you will keep in touch with the White Lodge.

Your testing in obedience to this rule will come constantly while you take part in the social life around you You are in the Kali Yuga, the characteristic of which age is the intensity of the strife on the physical plane Not alone is there conflict among the races of man in their national ideals, thus making for great wars , but also in the smaller cycle within the greater Yuga,—there is within every nation an ever-increasing discord between capital and labour, autocracy and democracy, youth and age, man and woman, respect for legal enactments and anarchy.

Again, in the sphere of religion, there is dissension between liberal and conservative, hierarchial and individualistic, orthodox and heterodox, anthropomorphic and Universalistic, formalistic and iconoclastic, dogmatic and free-thinking

Free yourself from prejudice and see clearly that all this activity is divinely good. It is an expression of the age-long contest between those Cosmic Rivals—Brahma, the creator, Vishnu, the conserver, and Shiva, the destroyer The One Life of the Universe, to maintain manifestation, shows itself forth as threefold Each is necessary to both the others, all are necessary to the evolution of man Masters and disciples of the White Lodge are in all three of these activities. Yet you are asked and will find it necessary to decide according to your temperament in which form of energy you will best help mankind.

You will be tempted, because of the magnetic affinities engendered by taking birth in a particular nation, to favour that nation and its welfare more than the welfare of the total race To feel this patriotism is extremely valuable in the middle stages of evolution It is right and absolutely essential to the higher and fuller growth of personality.

It is the spring from which flow noble deeds, acts of self-forgetfulness, and, if the national ideal be high, the men and women of that state will be blessed in this feeling. You, however, are now at the point where you must sever your attachments, you must view the whole Human Race with love and understanding You must work with the ideal that seems high and true to you wherever it appears.

To develop this power of seeing the welfare of the total humanity, without personal or national predilection, you should read and study " The Secret Doctrine," by H. P. Blavatsky. This book, more than any other in the English Language, will enable you to become a true world-thinker and a clear-seeing observer of human life

You will find yourself equally tempted to become entangled in the religious controversies of your time. Temperamentally you will cleave to one expression and be prejudiced against other tendencies and statements If you are naturally a free-thinker and hold that freedom of individual self-determination is needful to true evolution, you are likely to be violently antagonistic to dogma and theological creeds , you will hate ritualism and stereotyped forms of devotion, you will look upon priesthood, especially if associated with political power, as a menace, and priests as enemies to the spiritual life in man. If you are naturally conservative you will look upon this same priesthood in the light of a backbone supporting the emotional social body-politic You will consider mankind as a child, unable to govern itself and needing many nursery tales. You will sympathise with the priests in their assumption of authority over " the masses." If they use this authority for political ends you will not see it as anything alarming or antagonistic to the best interests of mankind You will believe in the rule of hierarchies, and will probably have little sympathy with democratic institutions You will look upon them as the froth of a turbulant sea—the undeveloped and uncontrolled rabble.

Again, you may be a mystical idealist, with a natural outpouring of rich devotion to some personality, whom you conceive as a saviour, and in the honouring and adoring of whom you find joy and peace In this case you will be inclined to let yourself be swept into some vortex of sectarianism and devotiousness to some personified ideal. You will love the symbol as such, and are not likely to desire the philosophical meaning behind it, since to discern that would be to destroy the joy and satisfaction of personal adoration You will find your religious aspirations fulfilled by the homage to Jesus, Sakyamuni, Krishna, or Maitreya This predisposition to adore personality is also characteristic of many who think they are approaching and pleasing the masters of the White Brotherhood by prostrating themselves and assuming an attitude of inferiority. No Master of Wisdom is ever flattered or charmed by sycophancy At the most he is tolerant to what may be a true ideal for certain unevolved highly emotional men and women Devotiousness is not true devotion (Bhakti)

The true aspirant for whom this rule is written must rise above these three expressions of religious life—free-thinking, conservative-orthodoxy, and mystical-idealism Each has its place and fulfils an important function in the spiritual unfolding of man You will probably feel that you want to work in the religious sphere, as you do in the political realm, but you must so work without any sense of separative superiority You must realise that each ideal is true, and may develop nobility, though none in itself is noble The sincerity of the one who therein expresses his life alone ennobles it

In the same impersonal way you must view the strife between capital and labour, remembering that the selfishness of the poor man is in no way superior to the selfishness of the rich, nor do the Masters o Wisdom count the worth of a man by the amount of money that he controls or the place he fills in the social life of the community The Masters value a man for his attitude to his fellow man in whatever circumstance he may be, and by his meeting the responsibilities imposed upon him by his station A Master may love a socialist agitator who is so because of a burning desire to help the downtrodden, but we may be sure that he does not love that element in so many socialist agitators which makes them what they are merely because they covet their neighbour's palace or other symbol of wealth A Master may love the capitalist who looks upon himself as a steward and who sincerely wishes to spend his resources for the education and betterment of mankind, but he certainly does not love that ostentation which gives large sums to charity and public benefactions through self pride and a desire to increase his sense of personal aggrandisem t.

In viewing human life you must know in every case that it is the
spirit only that quickeneth.   To be poor in worldly goods is not in
itself a virtue nor is the possession of monetary wealth a vice.   The
" poverty " in occultism is to have a sense of non-possession in whatever environment, rich or poor, knowing that whatever you seem to
possess belongs to humanity for its service

In like impersonal manner you will view the struggle between
man and woman, youth and age, the retrospective idealist and the
pioneer into the far future, you will love them all and develop
sympathy with them in their various ideals, striving to comprehend
the terms in which each defines life

■ ■ ■ ■ ■

RULE IX.

Become indifferent to objects of perception.

NOTE that this rule does not tell you to cultivate aversion to objects
of perception   It does not make of asceticism, as we in the West
use the word, a virtue

As you follow this rule you must cultivate the capacity to act as
the duty of the day determines, neither looking to the reward, nor
shrinking from the pain which may be karmically inherent in the
action   To continually perform all actions in this manner is to have
developed the true " indifference to objects of perception "

In the world of sensuous experience, pleasures and pains are
necessary.   They are called in the Gita, " The contacts of the senses."
They come and go, impermanent   In themselves they possess neither
virtue nor its opposite   The true path does not lie in choosing one
and excluding the other, but in accepting both as you accept the other
phenomena of nature—rain and sunshine, etc   When you have
reached the point when you carry out your ideal without being affec-
ted by either pleasures or pains, then you have mastered this ninth
rule

Realize clearly, however, that in the life of discipleship you are
not going to free yourself from either pleasures or pains   You will
experience both, but your attitude to them will differ entirely from
that of the average man

Know also that the objects of perception are on all four of the form levels of your consciousness, and hence you must be indifferent to the pleasures and pains of life, whether on the lower physical, the higher physical, in the Kama-Loka, or in Devachan Your ideal of human service carries through them all

Of course the indifference here referred to applies to your own pleasures and pains, not to those of humanity whom you serve

In order to reach this indifference you must give a true value to the senses, neither minimising nor over-estimating their importance. Western philosophy and science are so materialistic in the present age that the empirical sensuous experience has assumed a place out of all proportion to its true worth. Remember it has true worth and very great value in the cosmic education. When in your occult life as a servant you are told to subjugate the senses, realize clearly that your task is to free yourself from this over-emphasis. It is good discipline to refrain from the gratification of the senses, from time to time, but do not come under the illusion that there is any particular virtue in this abstinence It is merely a means to an end, never an end in itself. Self-control means the control of the senses by the Self , it does not mean that you refrain from doing your duty through fear of sensuous pleasure.

■ ■ ■ ■ ■

RULE X.

Approach the Masters

By the time you, the disciple, have put into practice the fore-going rules you will be prepared in your mind to accept the fact that you are not the ultimate examples of human knowledge, and that beyond you are the Great Companions, human beings whose minds are mighty storehouses of science, philosophy, and the laws of being, compared to which your knowledge is as a wax candle to a great search-light.

Furthermore you will have developed a humility which will clearly show you that your love and compassion are still darkened by selfishness, and are pale shadows of that glowing ideal of perfect sympathy which you picture in your heart. You will have no difficulty in accepting the fact that these great knowers and lovers exist in the world of m n You will not any longer battle against the nomenclature Masters of Wisdom, Masters of Knowledge, and Masters of Compassion when applied to these comrades and perfect embodiments of the purpose to which your own life is becoming consecrated

Just here let me quote H P Blavatsky's words from a letter " Woe will *certainly* follow that man who denies to the Masters of Wisdom physical forms, and, placing them apart from humanity, makes them objects of worship "

How shall we approach the Masters ?

By following the nine rules already laid down and by realizing further that as you develop some particular ideal of human perfection and try to make it manifest in the outer humanity you will inevitably draw to yourself that Master whose ideal is nearest your own. He has been working for ages at that dharma which you are now beginning. This Master will help, strengthen, enlighten, and reveal to you whole vistas of power, and means to the end you desire. This is the beginning of your preparation for your first major initiation

Each initiation of the candidate is followed by a wider and deeper view of the human problem.

Various illuminations called minor initiations, may and undoubtedly will come to you while following the first nine rules, but your whole life is now preparing for a change such as the undedicated man cannot conceive.

To approach the Masters you must know absolutely that the Lord of Life is in your own heart, and hence in the heart of all that lives. The true life-consciousness within you is the Supreme Lord in all forms , but this knowledge, or Yoga of the Universal Reality, must not become a mere arrogant apperception You must realize this Supreme Reality, while at the same time, as a servant, you recognize under time's limitations the growth, evolution and the cycles of ever-unfolding perfection

To attain to the first major initiation of the White Lodge it is not sufficient for you to know yourself to be God, one with the Infinite Godhead—unlimited by anything in time or space—you must pierce the *meaning* of Maya and become *consciously* that part of the Godhead which governs the existence and the manifested universe. You must, while perceiving yourself as the infinite and immutable TAT (That), yet plunge fearlessly into the world of illusion and work with the law of Karma. You must now put consciously into operation your knowledge of the forces of Nature, using your whole personality only as an instrument in a cosmic task.

Arrived here it becomes imperative under occult law that the Master of Wisdom guarding and protecting that ideal which you have made your own, reveal himself to you in an intimate way as your Co-Worker and Elder Brother. You will before this have over-passed pride and vanity, and human service alone will possess you.

Shall you now appear as a saint, or the embodiment of the conventional ethical standard of goodness of the church and the world of the time? Not necessarily! You may appear outwardly to be just that—or equally, you may appear to be the reverse. It is not the outward garment of seeming that counts in the workers of the White Lodge. Pioneers and prisons are often well acquainted Christs and crucifixions are proverbial "The highest virtue is always hidden," says a great Master, and since you have undertaken to identify yourself with the total of humanity you will be indifferent to social respectability if it come between you and your task.

. . . . .

INTERPOSAL.

WE will now assume that for seven years you have been practising concentration with the continuous dedication of your whole being to the service of man.

This Ideal has thus become the guiding power and determining impulse of your life

You are accepted

You have overcome the temptations and obstacles placed before the outer personality, you have taken the vow of obedience to your own Inner God—that you will obey unswervingly the Voice of the Silence, your inner spiritual realization of right in the performance of the duty imposed upon you by your own ideal of human service.

You have taken the vow of poverty, which is that you will not hold anything as belonging to the personality apart from the well-being of the human race, since the personality and all that pertains to it has been *given* to the ideal of human service. You have laid down your life and the Spiritual Law has begun to operate. In taking the vow of poverty you have come to realize that personal

possessions are not alone money and worldly goods, but also your
accomplishments, achievements, endowments, talents, capacities,
powers and all *karmic rewards* for past endeavour   All these you
have laid on the doorstep of the shrine, and your Inner Self dwelling
in the hearts of all men has accepted your offer   By abandoning all
sense of personal possession you have identified yourself with this
Self and dwell in conscious union with It

You have taken the vow of chastity—that is, you have decided
to view your body as a temple of the Living Self—pure, and in all
its organs and parts acceptable   You have recognised that it is
what comes forth from a man's heart that degrades or exalts him,
and you have therefore determined to project and maintain a physical
form adequate to the growing needs of mankind   As a servant
dedicated to the continuous life of man, you are not trying to leave
the physical body behind you, but to keep it as a clean, pure, strong,
vibrant, healthy, efficient and complete instrument for service
You have recognized that each man is self-responsible and self-
determinative, and ordains absolutely his own future, whether for
good or for ill   This recognition has left you clear of all exoteric,
covenant religions, with their conceptions of external atonements,
outer Golgothas, names whereby you may be saved, etc   There
is no Saviour except the living power of Truth and Love within
each man's own heart   The Saviours, so-called, are those men and
women, who through love and truth, have come to the knowledge
of the Oneness of all men, the Eternal and Immortal Life   Their
words then, point to the path which if any man will follow, he may
save himself, for each man must save himself from the bondage
and illusion of his own personality.   Yet these saviours all unite in
stating that no man can save himself who seeks to do so, but only
by losing himself for the salvation of others

True chastity is to look upon the creative functions and sexual
organs and powers of the bodies of all men and women with the same
purity and cleanness as that with which you view the budding of the
leaves, the opening of the blossoms, the passing of the bees from flower
to flower, and all other forms of the fruitage and fecundity of the
Earth

You are *not* born in sin nor conceived in iniquity.

If your thoughts are wholesome, noble and true, then your creative power will fill you with health, and the children of your thoughts, your sexual emotions, and your bodies will also be children of Light and filled with physical and moral health.

You may wonder why I have not written these three vows as rules   It is because the problems underlying the taking of these vows arise at different times in the disciple's life   They may have come to you on the day of your first dedication.   They may have come together or separated by months or years   They may be, only now, at the end of your seven years probation, assuming the proportions of concrete and personal problems, which you must solve and conquer.

To be chaste, to be without any sense of personal possession, and to be obedient to the voice of your Inner Self—these are essential however, to your future progress from this point.

Now begin some of the testings of the inner man.   Among these you will find none more subtle and leading to greater confusion than that of supporting your physical life while carrying out the ideal to which your life is dedicated.   You have been steadily seeking the Kingdom of Heaven, the abode of the Self in the hearts of all men, and striving to develop its righteousness in all humanity   You have developed zeal and earnestness in your endeavour.   You would wish to give your whole time to the task—yet you find yourself in all probability with obligations to family or others, and do not feel that it is right for you to neglect them   In this you are right, but you are only right because your faith in the Eternal Purpose and the Great Plan is not yet what it will become as you continue your dedication and spiritual expansion.   It is a law absolute and unalterable that all your physical wants and needs, and these also of those seemingly dependent upon you will be met without any thought, effort, or care on your part *if your life be really given to the service of man.*

You need have no doubt on this point.   Seek ye first the kingdom of heaven and its righteousness, and everything that the personality needs to maintain its full capacity and usefulness will be given unto it abundantly, freely, and just as it is needed   Your environment will always be of the character best for your own development and for the work to which your heart is given.   You have a physical, emotional, mental and spiritual completion and expansion, because

these things are necessary to the fuller and deeper usefulness which
will be yours in the future.   You need have no fear.   If your dedication is sincere and continuous, these things will certainly be added
unto you.   It is not a matter of bargaining, you cannot give to get ;
you must give freely, without considering the return, though the
return is certain.

■ ■ ■ ■ ■

RULE XI.

Take no Remuneration for your Spiritual Work.

THIS rule applies to that section of the White Lodge which we
call the Pure Aryan.   In the White Lodge, composed as it is
of "the Servants of Mankind," there are various departments, and
their ideals, though always pertaining to human service, differ in
their outward form and statement.   I will now assume that the
Aryan Ideal is the one to which you wish your life to conform.
Your dedication will now become somewhat limited, appearing less
universal than heretofore. It will now take this form—

I, here and now, will that my life and whole personality shall be
devoted to the *intellectual* and *spiritual* unfoldment of man

You will note that by thus limiting yourself you have taken this
tremendous step in the occult life   You could not have taken this
step earlier, because if you had done so, it would have been at
the expense of your universal love and with a sense of superiority
and even arrogance towards other ideals for human well-being,
such as, for instance, the physical, emotional and psychic departments of evolution.   Now your love shows you that all these are
necessary and although you now restrict the field of your endeavour
to specialize on the intellectual and spiritual phases, it is with the
full recognition of the necessity of all the ideals of those who serve
mankind.   Later your ideal will again assume a more universal
character, but for a time this limitation is necessary.

To take no remuneration for your spiritual work becomes an
inviolable law in the Aryan section of the White Brotherhood
You simply are not allowed to ask for, or to take any salary,
stipend, wage or pay whatever for what you give of spiritual instruction or help   Gifts may, and undoubtedly will, be given to
you and may be accepted, but not as pay for your work   Never
must you ask for a reward or put a price on your free-giving   The

gifts of the Spirit are without money and without price. They are not yours except as you are a steward to the Universal Life If you think of them as your own or strive to make of them a source of revenue, or count them as marketable or something which you can exchange for a salary, then you are either a blind dupe of Folly or a thief and a robber Your spiritual vision will quickly fade and you will repeat dead formulae from which the life has departed. No paid speaker can be the custodian of the Living Word

This is why no true spiritual teacher in the Aryan Race is allowed to take pupils in an intimate way until his inner illumination has brought him the karma through which he may support his pupils while studying with him This opportunity to teach will come to you in time if you keep your dedication burning clearly, and strive against this temptation of the inner man. If you compromise on this matter you will delay your progress and limit your usefulness

As the phrase from Luke x 7, "The labourer is worthy of his hire," has been so often quoted as an excuse for taking money, it might be well for you to read the first twenty verses of that chapter and ask yourself if it is possible they could have been spoken by the Master Jesus, or whether they are not patently an interpolation by priestcraft No subterfuge of this kind is allowed. You cannot break this law. You had much better conquer the temptation now and clarify your mind on this matter before you go further

Of course, you understand that these rules are not written for the average man whose growth and development is still under the law of self-assertiveness, and who is battling in the market place to develop his self identity, but for those who have come under the latter law of self-renunciation, and whose lives have been laid down for the service of mankind This is what you have been doing for the last seven years in your morning and evening dedication Hence this rule is essential to you although it may not be applicable to others.

■ ■ ■ ■ ■

RULE XII.

Avoid Self-Pity.

As in Rule XI your problem was one pertaining to the struggle of the inner self, so here you have a similar subtle question to solve. Self-pity is one of the insidious temptations, because at this period of your development several years may pass while you are slowly ripening, in which there is no excitement. You are likely to appear abandoned The Masters seem to have lost sight of you You stand alone   Your capacities and talents, which you think valuable and wish to have used, seem to be ignored You see others given work and recognition, while you are left aside You chafe at the inertia.   You are tempted to throw yourself into movements which will flatter your personality Almost certainly you will compare yourself with others. You will begin to covet the opportunities of your comrades Envy, which you will not allow yourself to feel for the outer possessions and qualities of other men, inwardly pricks at your heart A dull, uncomfortable dissatisfaction blows as a mist through your psychic atmosphere. Introspection makes you hyper-sensitive to criticism The outer temptations which you overcame while becoming indifferent to objects of perception and to pleasures here or hereafter, now have to be interpreted as becoming indifferent to recognition at present or in the future If you know in your heart that your dedication to human service is complete and sincere; and to achieve this certainty is the first task you accomplish;—then you must learn to wait quietly until you are needed in the field for which you are being prepared The Masters of Wisdom know much better than you the place you hold in the larger plan. Struggle with self-pity. Remain apparently unperceived and be content Do not rush out into the so-called practical affairs of life, social movements, etc It may be quite right to work in these movements, but it is not right for you as a neophyte under training to use them as an anodyne to soothe your irritation or as an opiate to deaden the discomfort for your wounded pride

RULE XIII.

Avoid Ostentation.

GROWING from the same root as self-pity, and associated with the same subtle desire for recognition is the inclination to avoid and postpone the complete yielding of the self to the Self; to live on past reputation and to display your karmic gifts to those less developed in order to obtain their approval and adulation. It is pleasant to have the crowd admire you—even although to acquire this you have to sacrifice the esteem of your Higher Self and the approbation of those comrades of the Lodge more developed than are you.

You are forbidden to emphasise for this purpose any trick of personality. Your effort is to merge yourself in the life of your kind. You must not come out and stand apart   You must not put yourself on a pinnacle   Realize that any trick of attire, adornment, or mannerism used to separate you from the rest is not in harmony with the spirit of your dedication   It makes no difference whether it enhances or detracts from your appearance. If it make a separation between you and those around you—avoid it

The Master Lao Tse says :—"The great virtue is always unobtrusive "

Walt Whitman in his poem "The Answerer," has these words :—
"His welcome is universal—
He says indifferently and alike, How are you my friend? to the President at his levee
And he says, Good-day, my brother, to Cudge that hoes in the field.
And both understand him and know that his speech is right.
Here is our equal, appearing and new."

■ ■ ■ ■ ■

RULE XIV.

Beware of Self-Gratulation

MORE subtle still than self-display is the turning back on yourself for approbation when the darkness referred to in Rule XII comes on you.   You are prone to take refuge in the thought that it does not matter what others think of you, you know your own worth.   By doing this you attach yourself to an alien shore, and the great kindly currents of occult life, which were bearing you to the ocean of Immortality and Self-consciousness sweep past you leaving you stranded

. . . . .

RULE XV.

Avoid Self-Righteousness.

SUPPOSE now you have succeeded in conquering the temptation spoken of in the last three rules   You are likely to congratulate yourself upon your success, and the natural glow of pleasure may at once become a menace and a new temptation to be overcome. It is another phase of the self-gratulation of the preceding rule, and H P.B. said in speaking of it :—"A self-conscious virtue is the most damnable of all vices "

Before you became a candidate for the White Lodge and entered occultism, a good conscience was your best protection and a necessary friend and guardian to your life then among men.   Now you are under a different law, that which before was your chief instructor and guide must be put aside, since it tends to conserve and demarcate the personality from Alaya—the World Soul of Humanity   It must be lost as a part of that life that *must* be lost before the True Life is found.

RULE XVI.

Renounce all fruit of Action.

In order to be strong you must be one-pointed.   In order to be one-pointed you must have released yourself from all entanglements   Karma is the law of Action, that whatsoever is sown must be reaped

For the undedicated the same personality reaps as sows, but your life, being continually given in love to the betterment of man, is constantly sowing seeds, not from your own harvest, but for their well-being.   You have laid down your reward as a part of the personality which you have offered to the Cosmic Purpose You have now trained your mind to think for man's good without considering yourself in the process and a curious fact appears. As the personality is completely surrendered it becomes more defined and stronger, while at the same time self-interest fades away.

Dedicate your life continually to human service and do not shrink from the censure and criticism of those who do not see with your vision   Dread no failure, court no success, free yourself from fear of pain, and do not act with hope of reward   In this way you will be more useful and will erect no barriers against the stream of the Universal Life

. . . . .

RULE XVII.

Speak Truth! Act Truth! Be Truth!

In an earlier rule the quality of Truth was stated to be in the human heart.   It is not to be found in the fact of outer appearance, whether scientific, philosophic, or religious alone.   It is in yourself, a deep and abiding quality, and is the only saviour from the bondage of un-truth and illusion.   That is why all the so-called "sins" are worked out and "forth-given" except the sin against the Spirit of the Truth within.

There are THREE which witness within each man —

      (1) The Will-to-Truth, which is the Father-Mother of Spiritual Consciousness,

      (2) The developed quality of Truth—which is the only Spirit of Wisdom, and

(3) The same Spirit embodied in his actions that makes of man the Son of the Eternal, who is the Alone-Begotten of this Eternal Spirit of Truth within his own heart

Make no mistake on this point

The priesthoods of this world continually strive to bamboozle the people and to distort and veil this One Great Reality

Give this quality full play within you. Develop the Will-to-Truth. Be fearless in your expression of Truth as you see it If your Will-to-Truth be sincere then you will become embodied of Truth and will bring forth only the Children of Light.

Every Master of Wisdom, every Adept of the White Lodge is an embodiment of the Light, a perfect expression *in the physical form of man* of the glory of Truth The ETERNAL SPIRIT and CONSCIOUSNESS of the world is served *only* in this Spirit of Truth. It is never external to a man, but is always and only found within.

The Kingdom of Heaven is within. Its gates open outward. They may be preserved from rust by constant usage The Will-to-Truth which is the Father-Mother who dwells in the Kingdom of Heaven, holds their key and releases the Holy Spirit which alone can save man from error Truth shining forth, guided by Love to mankind, becomes Wisdom There is no right usage of knowledge which has not this quality of Truth—with Love as its guide

. . . . .

RULE XVIII.

Be Yourself the Speaker in all Scriptures as you read Them

YOU will find, as a dedicated servant of man, that you are united with the *Eternal,* and that all scriptures point finally to that state of consciousness which *you* have attained by your dedication to Truth and Love.

"Look inward, Thou art Buddha "

"The Tao dwelleth in You, and goeth forth to the whole universe."

"Ye are the Fire which burns the dross and leaves the pure Gold "

"The Kingdom of Heaven is within You "

Ye search the scriptures that in them ye shall find *your true Self*, for You are THAT of which all scriptures teach

You are the Christ and the Power of the Word speaks through all Your utterances in the great Scriptures.

You have laid down your life and have found Yourself

Not alone should you unite Yourself with the sayings of the saviours, knowing that they are Your Own Voice, but You should also realise that all the philosophers have sprung from the same *Mind* and are expressions through other personalities of Your' evolutionary thinking

Yield to no embodied master control of Your life

Seek not for your master in the world of form, physical, astral, or mental. Realise always that the power for Righteousness dwells in yourself, never in externals.

Love your comrades in the Cosmic Work, but never adore or worship them

·····

RULE XIX.

Be Free.

You have loved imprisonment You have shrunk from responsibility in the Spiritual Kingdom—yet only in the taking of the responsibility imposed upon you by *your* inner highest Ideal (your dharma) can you be free

Love to mankind and the Service of Truth has raised your consciousness above all barriers.

You will be told by those of lesser vision that you must obey, reverence, and show devotion to an external power, before whom you must humble yourself, and whom you must serve This is a lie There can be no compromise on this matter. Be free from bondage by the Spirit of Truth, and the glory of that spirit shall dwell in you and around you.

RULE XX.

Avoid Stunts.

I HAVE adopted this current slang because I find no English equivalent   Stunts include :—

(1) Spectacular exercises (whether performed in public or in private) ;

(2) Experimental parades, and

(3) Set abnormal tests, whether of breathing or posture.

The Great Spiritual Quest and the Paths thereof are extremely simple.   A Child need never err therein.   Dedication to the Service of Mankind and a constant unswerving use of your whole manhood and womanhood to this ideal are all that is essential.

We find, however, very few who are willing to live by simplicity, and very many who measure their occult development by the growth of abnormal powers.   You may have psychic powers, emotional expansion, and mental capacity, and yet be far from Wisdom and from brotherhood in the White Lodge

I am not now referring to things done from ostentation and to win the applause of the crowd.   I am warning you against an error into which, with the best intentions, you may easily fall.

There are many occult schools, most of which are devoted to the cultivation of egoism and the strengthening of " Tannha "— *t.e* , the thirst for personal experience and growth.

He who will save his life shall lose it   He who wills to lose his life in the service of Mankind shall find the Cosmic Life flow through him.

• • • • •

RULE XXI.

Love Simply   Do Not Fear to Love

You will be met by men apparently wise, who will tell you that love to humanity is an error, and by cultivating this love you are submerging yourself more deeply in maya (illusion) They will say '' Humanity is a very temporary form of the Universal Life,'' and that '' the Wh te Lodge,'' who live only to serve it, are bound to a form of illusion and blinding themselves to reality.'' They will tell you that you should be free from all love, all attachment to form, and should separate yourself from the world of form entirely They will say that love and hate equally bind man to error Their argument is that it is through pain and suffering that man returns to his true spiritual kingdom, and that all compassion and sympathy shown to man tend to perpetuate the condition of human bondage. '' Therefore,'' they say, '' you should renounce all pity, and all help to man and beast, and should never identify yourself or admit your relationship to family, race, or other form in time and space.'' They say that Life-Consciousness is Eternal, and that which is manifested to the Seer (Purusha) is temporal and evanescent, hence You, as the Eternal Thinker, should never attach Yourself by love or compassion to any form.

The fallacy of this argument lies in the assumption that Love is one in a pair of opposites. This is untrue. Love is eternal, and its operation is the basis of all manifestation. The Song of Life is Joy, not as they assert, pain. Desire and aversion are the opposites, Love is above any opposite

It has been the method of the White Lodge to leave a very great deal to the intuition of the candidate at this point, but owing to the tremendous development of psychic power and the expansion of knowledge in the psychic sphere (*equally materialistic with the physical*) it is well that certain hints should be given to you as an index to the True Path through the "Hall of Learning" (*vide* "Voice of the Silence," H.P B.).

Strangely enough, however, this school referred to above, which is supposed to teach utter indifference to all forms, has yet an elaborate system of stunts, which it will put before you in the name of *Advaita, Shiva Rudra,* or *Parameshin.* They are intended to free you from the bondage of illusion, and to lead you to rest in the bosom of the Eternal and Uncontaminable Formless Essence of Pure Being.

From the foregoing I do not wish you to assume that exercises in concentration are superfluous. All I wish you to realise is that stunts in themselves will not lead you on the True Spiritual Path. The cultivation of the instrument for the larger purpose is, of course, necessary

Another school which will confront you with subtle arguments is that which teaches that since the life of the Universe is one it can make no difference what action you perform, and that all ideals in the world of time are equally binding, and, therefore, equally without value. This school will say, "Cast yourself down into the abyss of darkness. The Life of the Supreme is everywhere, and whatever you do you are serving some aspect of this Life. Therefore do not define or limit your dharma in any direction. Serve the Abyss, which is the Supreme."

Members of this school will tell you that this is a wider and nobler ideal than the service of man. The fallacy of this statement lies in *the fact that without specific limitation of will no concrete manifestation of the Universe could take place,* and the Divine plan could never be built in outer forms. Your duty as a human being is to serve the Supreme Life in humanity and to make objective the Great Plan revealed to you through your dedication to that service.

The whole of humanity is now evolving. There are no human beings called upon to involve themselves more deeply into matter, though there are many who must lose the fear of the flesh in order to develop the body for the Cosmic evolutionary purpose. "The cessation of sins and faults is not for deva (building) egos." This school teaches also hypnotism and the cultivation of passive mediumship Now, there is a rule in the Aryan White Lodge that none of its members shall allow himself to hypnotise or to be hypnotised either on the physical or astral plane. Passive mediumship in trance condition is merely hypnosis from the astral plane into the physical and is forbidden. Hence, avoid all actions which tend to make you passive and non-self-responsible (vide Rule IV. on "Concentration.")

A third school teaches that rigid asceticism is the path leading to Wisdom and argues that by hatred of the flesh and by despising all bodily desires one returns to the heavenly kingdom, and therefore stunts are ordained by it through which, it claims, a man becomes free from fleshly desires. The fallacy of this school is that the flesh is thought of as an evil and foul prison instead of "a winged palace of joy " Self control of the body is not only good, but necessary, but the practice of self-control should be not with aversion to the body, and the refraining from sensuous experience is only a means to an end and not, in itself, a virtue. This school contends that hatred and fear of the body is self-control. This is a mistake. Fear of the flesh is (really) bondage to the flesh.

You must become indifferent to the flesh and to objects of perception, being swayed neither by aversion to outer experience nor by attachment to the forms of sensuous experience.

■ ■ ■ ■ ■

RULE XXII.

Become the "Son of Man"

AND now we come to the final rule—You have realised that behind your life lies a great purpose, and have made yourself, by constant dedication, a servant of the whole of humanity You have widened your vision and deepened your sympathy so that now you are able to become a child of man

You are ready for birth from the human, into the human—for although you will be born out of the strife and turmoil of the personal conflict you will not separate yourself from the strife and tumult of your less enlightened brethren of the human family You will not strive to run away from man into some world of deep forgetfulness, you will keep your heart as an open channel of love to all your little ones, "the blind Orphan—humanity"— whose life you have made your own by identification through the ideal.

You have realised the great secret of sex, that whatever is in the mind in the sexual act becomes stronger for good or ill and hence you no longer degrade the channels of life into form by unclean, shameful, ignoble and wholly selfish thinking. Your sex is used with purpose in the larger plan and you view your body as a temple of the living God in all its parts and organs, holy, pure and acceptable   There is no longer a strife between the flesh and the Spirit. You have perceived the need of a wide emotional sympathy, hence you no longer starve your "feeling" nature.

You have recognised your responsibility, and the power of your thought, therefore you do not depict idle and undirected imaginations, but build clearly images in your mind for the well being of humanity in freedom, joy and beauty. You perceive that sensuality is the selfish, undirected and purposeless indulgence of the senses; hence you avoid it and strive to help others also to overcome this error

Your whole being belongs to mankind for its service and you are ready to take a great step into the Mystic Brotherhood of the White Lodge.

Nothing that is human repels you, you enter with sympathy and understanding into the solving of all the perverted complexes due to man's ignorant thinking. You will not accept anything that all may not have on equal terms, "all bitter condemnation dies." You realise the meaning of certain essential statements—"Judge not and ye shall not be judged, condemn not and ye shall not be condemned, with what measure ye mete it shall be measured to you again." You have risen above the religious implication of these words into what is infinitely more important, the psychological perception of their truth and value

You must be prepared to stand alone, though never were you so closely knit as now with the Great Ones of the world.

In giving your messages you are likely to be cast from the churches, societies and congregations of men. You will be rejected and dispised, taunted and vilified by those to whom you have given your very life-blood—but this shall be your certificate of worth, for ever so have all the sons of men in their love to mankind been treated. Misunderstanding, lies and innuendo will surround you as a garment wherever you go.

You will be hated by all the self-righteous and those who rest upon the conventional moralities of the time, yet you shall "walk the whole world over, free." Living in eternity you shall not be concerned with the midges of temporal irritation. The garden of peace filled with beauty will stretch for boundless leagues on either side the *Open Road,* on which your feet are treading

You will know the Great Companions and will carry signs and tokens unmistakable, but you must call no man Master—since there is only one Master—the Eternal Life through all the forms of the Universe—the Life in your own heart in full consciousness of its unlimited nature.

You tread the Path because you have become the Path, you hear the Voice of the Silence, because you are Yourself the Speaker. You speak in the presence of the Masters because all men have become supremely dear to you, and hence you cannot wound though you may have to stimulate them

And so, in closing this little book, written and dedicated to all lovers of men, I invoke upon you, also so dedicated, the peace and wisdom, the power and purity of the Great White Lodge, the Eternal Brotherhood and Sisterhood of Light, wearing the physical forms of men in the outer world of darkness and ignorance I invoke anew the revealing of the Universal Mind in Whose depths is held the plan, which in our building we all follow, and I invoke also the Spirit of the Earth our Mother, that she may bless your bodies and your creative functions in the three fields of your soul—physical, emotional, and mental.

I will you, oh, my Comrades, that you unite ever more fully as the milleniums roll with the total human family, holding as your motto —

> Take me not, Lord, until—Nay!—Until when?
> Not till I bring with me one heart, one mind,
> Thine every little one, and pray that then,——
> If one must stay, I may be left behind

PEACE BE WITH YOU.

The End.

Lightning Source UK Ltd.
Milton Keynes UK
UKHW020626240522
403447UK00005B/356

9 781376 947724